PLENITUDE

Thomas McCarthy was born in Cappoquin, Co. Waterford, in 1954 where he was educated at the local Convent of Mercy and subsequently at University College Cork. He worked for many years at Cork City Libraries before retiring to write full-time in 2014. He was a Fellow of the International Writing Program, University of Iowa in 1978–79 and International Professor of English at Macalester College, Minnesota, in 1994–95. He is a member of Aosdána, the Irish Assembly of artists and writers. He has won several awards for his poetry, including The Patrick Kavanagh Award, the Alice Hunt Bartlett Prize, the O'Shaughnessy Prize and the Ireland Funds *Annual Literary Award*. His first collection, *The First Convention,* was published by The Dolmen Press, Dublin, in 1978 and his most recent collections, *Pandemonium* (2016), and *Prophecy* (2019), were published by Carcanet Press. A former Editor of *Poetry Ireland Review* and *The Cork Review,* his journals, *Memory, Poetry and the Party,* were published by The Gallery Press in 2022 and his essays, *Questioning Ireland,* appeared in 1924. He lives in Cork with his wife, the photographer and heritage gardener Catherine Coakley, and they have two adult children, Kate Inez and Neil.

PLE

THOMAS

NIT

McCARTHY

UDE

CARCANET POETRY

First published in Great Britain in 2025 by
Carcanet
Main Library, The University of Manchester
Oxford Road, Manchester, M13 9PP
www.carcanet.co.uk

A CIP catalogue record for this book is
available from the British Library.

ISBN 978 1 80017 410 8

Book design by Andrew Latimer, Carcanet
Typesetting by LiteBook Prepress Services
Printed in Great Britain by SRP Ltd, Exeter, Devon

The publisher acknowledges financial
assistance from Arts Council England.

CONTENTS

PLENITUDE

A MEADOW IN JULY

It's just that a poem is forming a meadow
For itself. And then a window –
Not a modern window at all but an old, flaking
Casement thing, ropes and pulleys

And weights you could hear
Banging inside their unpainted timber frames.
The deepest thing has a rumble
That you can never see,

A distant thunder in a thundery July;
The way poems heave in their nervousness
Before small birds hit the windows,
Thinking poetry is a drift of insects

Or some such promise of food.
We gaze beyond our rooms in idleness,
Idly dreaming of things outside ourselves,
A full plate that we intuit

Before we come to our senses
In that hide-out the poem has made
Between our faces and July. See, it's the same poem
Has placed glass between us and a meadow.

THE ONE LEAF

Here beneath a tree time will tell
Whether it was worth getting up this morning,

Though none of us are immune.

The self that time makes worthwhile
May never seem whole
In the way Samuel Beckett was
With that one single leaf
On the tree of his entire life:

His bitter truth is not cinnamon, nor should it be.

If time doesn't want to have faith
Or absorb any scripture
There is simply nothing that can ever be done
With the leaf on the tree or the lost leaf.

Let me be plain about this and never emotional

Because time will tell: there is a purple shellac
Of the one leaf from the crushing of beetles,
And still a holy rood within. It's just that time,

A leaf, always has the last word.

PARALLEL

in memory of Christo

Echoes, more than anything else create a way in,
Like when yer man wrapped the Reichstag in folds and draperies

And made it seem, momentarily, a tender thing.
The way sunlight fell on it made a sound

Of your heart beating.

Similarly, when we walked under his saffron gates
In Central Park we were young again;

And it was the same when I heard the glottal words
Uttered by that Irishman's oily purples and greens,

All of his parallel lines like so much sheet music,

A music that deprivation makes
With a heavy lid upon it for too long –

Again, I ask you what Art is. As I did

When I held your fingers, outstretched. Your engagement ring,
I remember, against my finger created an echo, an ekphrastic.

LATE SUMMER

A butterfly wing, to begin with.

The incongruous remnant of a life
Colourised by an aching summer

And a fullness in each hour.
Now a wing devoid of the living thing

That gave it meaning:
The way this empty kitchen speaks

Of the heavy cargo, the Irish miles
Chased down by swallows.

Architecture makes novelists of us.
Rooms bear a coffin that will not be silent

But ache to share with us their deaths
Within. When the dead speak

It's as if a young professor
Newly hired had fallen overboard

With all the notes from Anglo-Irish life
Washed in the swell and lost.

This mansion sips from its own reflection
In late autumn loneliness. Its lawns and patios

Lean back, opening a wet mouth.

THE ART OF FIXING A SHADOW

for Clíona Ní Ríordáin

A host of beech stems in late winter, with little food
In the light: their silver nitrates are fixed in my memory now
As on a spattered parchment. A cold Rochester graveyard
And I at de Valera's mother's grave, neither inside nor
Outside my life at that moment, but floating in spoors
Of dust that seemed to drift from the strange day –
Memory tries to be a frank revelation of the commonplace,
It tries so hard for the vernacular formula, seeking empathy
And warmth from the surface that it is impressed upon.
I was once a person who remembered differently; what
Seemed heroic then is now but a pitiful thing, all belief gone
And the politics of that. Such a childhood I've had, it was
Always running towards an obdurate adult, always keen
To be settled in a lithographic varnish or in adult resistances
Made of tar or asphaltum. Time has dissolved these childish
Oils of lavender. If memory has framed time-consuming
Details they were never reliable, memory's astonishing
Fidelity is merely to itself. Come to think of it, it wasn't
Beech stems at all, that time in America, it was really the bare
Red stems of Dogwood, a wintering flame of Cornus
Sanguinea, blazing in low sunlight in a less than lucid moment
Of impressions. Too late to fume the plates over iodine
Crystals, to begin the process of re-remembering. From the
Collodion negative of what happens, we cut and turn,
We bathe and hope to dry. And the poem, in its own strict
Chemical sense, it is our one fixed carbon or albumen print.

IMMORTAL FORM IN THE MARGINS OF SEAN SCULLY'S 'JOHN ANTHONY'

Time on the margin, on the edge or the between of things,
Pours across the heavier breath of these oils, flows between
Grey and darker fields as a mouse made of light, a shrew
Caught feverishly in a stretch of subdued linen. My mind has
To be un-made in the way this linen was that became a field
For art, a slope, a precipice. If I could fly I would attempt this
Cliff-face of the heart, what's insecure; an attempt such as that.
I am here for the long ride and hanging in as my mind sets oil
Scurrying across fields of lesser light, harvests of primed cloth.
It is nothing if not narrow, this possibility of life in the margins
Between the fullness of grey, the fullness of off-white, the
Assertions of black, of black's heavy black brushwork. Avian
Is the effort of paint, a crow, a tumbler-pigeon attempting air,
Crashing wing-long into hardness. A surface is self-educated
And its auto-didactic heart is art: here, the master-stroke and
All its minions. My eyes trace with their finger-tips this long
Voyage between settled land masses of paint, ocean-going
Fingers trace this surface of sunlight between black and grey,
Striations of white that end constantly in a sunburst, a breath
Of light. I turn a corner to find a chasm of yellow, all become
A stream of striations of white and yellow; and white again
In this brushwork ocean. Here is the hell of separation, of
Falls between outcrops of grey, of redemption in yellow again
And all those attempts at closing the gap between one form
Of coloured life and another. Here is a terrible storm, here
The empty and terrible void. The miserly brush has left
Us gasping for breath in its emptiness, its incompleteness
Between colours. Yellow the hope, or the promise of rest
In the failure of things to cohere. It is terrible, this art that

Leaves me with only a margin to depend upon, a vengeful
Subsistence of yellows and greys, the heaviness of things
Left yearning for cover. Here is a massive exposure of
Linen, of heaven un-primed and ill-prepared. Here is the cross
For art to bear, dove of Christ, tumbler tumbling through all
Absence of hope in the margins, as He was in the beginning.

AMARYLLIS

You are greedy for it, though where this feeling comes from
After an excess of Christmas, that mid-winter arc of eating,

Is a mystery to all who might be reasonable. After all,
There is this one astonishing Amaryllis flooding our room
With its reddish light, its sculpted, *Vogue*-like being

As if the seasons in our house were a catwalk, a parade.
But now I've just seen an array of tall, rare snowdrops
In my neighbour's conservatory, well-lit by the tissue

Of her tall lanterns, all of my neighbour's bounty glowing
At the end of this January day. I have been stalking catlike
For a better look. It is an excess of loveliness, delicate

As light through fine porcelain. Yet why should I lust
After some other richness when an Amaryllis
As excessive as a pier-glass of Murano craft fills

My life already with its own delicious luxury? It is
The depressing thing in our nature, surely? This never
To be satisfied. This yearning after the other, the new –

Just when life, that faithful and constant lover, has left
The bedroom for a moment carrying in a jar the spent year.

THE PROMISE OF SNOW

Snow on the mastheads of *Hotspur* magazine for boys,
Snow in the promise of things as December days darken
And bulky Christmas numbers accumulate around Miss Fraher:
This snow has taken hold of both of us as we cut
Through the straw-y, awkward binding-twine that binds
The late Christmas Eve train deliveries of *The Telegraph*
From the Holyhead ferry or the *Evening Press*
Via Limerick Junction. It is not the snows of yesteryear
Because we are both too damn busy for that, not
Yesteryear at all but mammon's fabulously evocative
Signal that the humanism of the newspaper trade
Has taken on a Christ-like frosting at this time of year.
The Christ in Miss Fraher's rickety old cash-register
Pings and pings with priestly insouciance, and I, like any
Good shepherd, have just been caught unawares
In the middle of this hardly surprising late December task;
So surprised, indeed, that I kneel continuously and praise
The flaky mangers of every village door. It is good news
We bring, and good news it is beneath this tinselled frieze
Of snow that falls into every isolated hallway at the top
Of every frozen boreen, or in the town's rain-soaked quarters.
We have portioned these bulky Christmas numbers into a series
Of manageable runs for a small boy; the two of us
Fallen into this frantic Christmas Eve together, wanting more
Than anything else in life to deliver just a promise of snow.

CHRISTMAS EVE, 1963

My holy family was down on its December luck, but I was not

As I delivered a Christmas number of *The Daily Mail*
To Miss Cliffe whose father had first reported upon
Our Blessed Lady at Knock. Christmas had come again without fail
As I knew it would. It was one of the eternal promises
Of Fianna Fáil that even the poorest might avail
Of Christmas: maybe even more than once a year, given
The way our Tariff Economy was booming. Light traces

Of snow peppered my fairly worn hand-me-down coat,
My knuckles were cold with a cold that wouldn't go
Away until maybe 1972 or '73, so there would be ten years of it
From that blue afternoon outside Miss Cliffe's door.
Being cold helps a child to concentrate on the strange sight
Of others being happy, houses where other children are not so poor.
I was living vicariously off Christmases seen behind glass

Like one of the Magi in the blue dark. Late, but nearer the light.

CONCERNING PROMETHEUS

My young father who was dying of a vengeful cancer called
to me from his death bed. I ran to him from that meadow
between two rivers, the Glenafallia and the Glenshelane, a
meadow where the gods shone with the radiance of my own
young limbs. My poor father, whom the gods didn't love, spoke
in urgent weariness:

1.

'Know these four old versions of the Promethean
Story. According to the first, your hero was chained
To a great rock in far-away Caucasian hills. Mr F. X.
O'Leary said he betrayed the secrets of the gods to men
And the gods sent eagles to feed upon his liver, the one
Part of him that renewed itself and renewed itself.

2.

According to the second legend, which I always
Thought was only a metaphor for cancerous pain,
Prometheus was stimulated by the eagles' beaks
Constantly tearing into his mortal flesh; goaded
He was, into pressing his own mortal frame deep
Into rock until he became one with the mountain.

3.

Be wary of the third legend before you begin
In poetry, of how his treachery was forgotten by
The gods over thousands and thousands of years;
How the gods forgot about this ancient treachery,
How the eagles forgot the liver and their flight-path;
Most of all, how even he forgot what he'd done.

4.

According to the fourth legend, all grew weary
Of the meaning of treachery. The gods in their
Idle eternity grew weary of a mere mortal liver,
The betrayer of secrets grey weary in his chains,
The eagles grew weary of meaningless torture;
Even the wound closed in its fleshly weariness.'

'I needed to speak with you,' he whispered, the breath of his lungs taken and wasted. 'Don't you worry about Prometheus,' my father explained, as he turned into the granite pillow where he prepared to die, 'it is the rock and the mountain you need to keep in mind today. It is a substratum of truth there-in, the one element inexplicable.'

D.V.

Burdens that the poor seemed to carry were lighter somehow
Between the will of God and the will of God. The hard rain

That fell slantways across your frayed coat, the blue snow
That made your delicate, girlish knuckles also blue; the pain

Of not knowing and never knowing how the house might appear
As you climbed the frightened, ungrateful tenement steps:

Such things were how God ventured, such things were in the fear
You felt for the lives of others and never your own life, except,

It must be said, in the days leading to Christ's day of birth;
Days when you thought, to the end of Advent, a turning of the key,

That something of Christ's peace might have landed on earth –
On your own house specifically. Worried, you might say,

Very quietly, "God willing, let's hope the mood is good inside.
Let's hope his mood has changed again." But flesh and state

Would be too weak to yield to our dreams; his crushing diatribes
Awaited your cold, ashen face. My hand in yours, I lost my faith.

THE REGENT INSTITUTE'S WRITE FOR PROFIT

'You will be glad to hear that I sold the short story I did for
Lesson 3 and have bought this typewriter with the proceeds.'
                                                          – A Student

You were the complete and absolute dreamer, dear father.
I salute you. You were simply marvelous. That you could leap
So far, like a shortwave signal leaping across darkened Europe,
And come back to earth, safely, for three days of thinning
Sugar beet on Jim Wall's farm, that was a sheer miracle of breadth –

So that as we sat like two children on the embankment
Above Cappoquin Station, watching Ireland bleed emigrants to death,
You wrote and rewrote with the stub of a Ballinamult Creamery pencil,
Private thoughts, purple and indelible as going without a full wage,

Reassured through a long winter of Nineteen Sixty-Two
That your Irish self was awaited by all 1,650 London editors.

This morning, in the fluorescent rain of sunlight and water,
I sheltered in a yellowy curvature of the dead patriot's house.
It excited me, for some daft reason, that a new business
Had just opened in the space where I sought to protect
My Saturdays newspaper. A Private Wealth company
Had placed its golden lettering across a plate-glass window:
Hard as rice, summer rain assailed its glassy shareholders.
I thought of James Merrill, who knew a thing or two about
Wealth – hardly common knowledge among poets, even now
In this era of creative industries. He wrote of 'The kiss of inky
Mafiosi' and the hope that he might delay in Florence. And still
The rich must cope with fruit and spinach, eggs and cheese,
In a Tuscan home of birdsong and half-resigned perfection.
For the rest of us it's the ennui of familiar rain, or sheltering
In the yellow porch of a restored house in a business district –
Us marvelling at persons who have more money than they need
To eat and travel, our disbelief that they might need advice.
We hoard issues instead of wealth; urgent issues fill up our coffers
With lustrous gold, newly minted. There is the issue
Of our young who cannot afford a home: there is no nest
For them in the places where they might begin to live. This
One issue burns a hole in the pocket of my brain, it creates
An unauthorised balance in the place where my soul
Should be at ease. It is every parent's worry: how will the young
Become if they cannot begin? And this rain that falls through a maze
Of sunlight, it has no answers at all, any more than the plaque
Behind me to a patriot who wrote one memorable ballad: such
Astonishing wealth across the block-chains of history!
I tried not to shelter too long in the one spot, restless
With a newspaper to read, my shoes beginning to take in water.
A suburban bus pulled in, shedding splashes, neither disgorging
Nor taking passengers aboard. But James Merrill's in my mind again
As I make a run for it in the rain. His shower of rice and petals.

25

APODICTIC

The absolute certainty of this evergreen shrub in its
Constant suffering, its struggle, makes me stand and listen.
'I won't undergo any therapy though I need it
After what I've been through': this scarlet Camellia
Speaks to me from its disturbed hovel between verdant
Laurel and viburnum tinus. Its tender attempts
At flowering in the teeth of wind are forgotten by me
Though its every leaf is tearful still, embittered by
The first frosts and fearful of what's to come. I try
To be lightly green and steady in its company, though
It is tragic to be born a Camellia in a land like ours.
Neither an indoor creature, nor a plant formed mentally
For the cold outdoors, it shivers in bitterness. If only –
If only I were as thoughtful as that retired army officer
Bringing Camellias indoors at just the right time,
Returning them to the garden wild before they die
Of thirst or heat, then there would be justice in this
World. Like most of us, they are happiest when a
Little obscured, not suffering fame directly or the sun
For too long. And that they need talking to is a
Given. And like most of us, they need company but not
Too much, need tenderness but not too much, need
A little disturbance at the roots, a walk across lawns
In a large tub. Knowing that summers don't last too long,
They want to feel unsettled in the way I am now disturbed
On a path between what is uncertainty and what is truth.

A BLUE BOOK TOKEN

With this Blue-Book Token I've decided to stay
With Miss Maria Edgeworth of Edgeworthstown
For the entire months of June and July. It's just
That my presumption is no worse than hers, or

No worse than any poor man kicked by a horse
At the tail end of a late winter Hunt; any man
Who upon recovering his consciousness in the
Splendid muck of a ploughed field beside a

Swinging gate thinks he might be a low-sized
Gentleman of the old school abandoned without
Even one post-Hunt champagne cocktail. If I
Presume to be a guest when I am only a Hunt

Follower closing gates at the end of a long day,
I am no worse than any Adventurer who took
Possession of these confiscated acres. The smell
Of crops burning, set on fire by a yeomanry

Of old, is still in my deepest thoughts as I trudge
Across the long grass of a margin, that margin
Of limes and elms, of beech hedge and laurel –
Enough, her butler's footsteps approach my desk.

MONTH OF THE DEAD

These broken stones of the year are everywhere
In the wet bracken of time, their crusty mussel-shells
Of each minute within. Such calm in the late moist air
Where November settles a moment, such thistles
In rotted rings, scutch-grass creating nests of decay.
Somewhere over the hill it will all begin again
But for now the entire year is twelve rolls of hay,
A larch, oak and ash wood silenced by weeks of rain.
I've come here not to observe without but within:
To call up life's accumulation the way my mother
Called upon assemblies of the dead around All Souls
And spoke to them as if they'd entered the kitchen
Just in time to be greeted by all the recalled others,
The sinners who did her wrong, the family fools –
A rosary-beads in her hand, she was among friends
Who were safely dead, who came to make amends

For all the times they'd left her on her own, so far
In her mind from Dungarvan where the electric lights
Shone, oh so isolated from the happier sisters
Who'd made marriages to conventional men. By rights,
That life should have been mine too, she'd complain
Between decades of rosaries, hypnotic *Hail Marys*
And end-of-chapter *Glorias*. Prayer was taking the strain
As this poem is now; not enough to hug the destinies
Her God had ordained, but to complain atheistically
As if Catholic prayer was one of God's local Deputies
Who'd deliver a stiff letter to the senior staff of Heaven.
Devoted to prayer, she thought it obvious for God to see
She'd been treated unequally. Here among wet trees
No sound from nature is her sound of getting even –
I can hear her plaintive weakness, its immense power,
Its millions of Irish faithful behind it. Belief like war.

Where November settles a moment, you'd think
Things might settle at my age. But what's unresolved
Is what's truly permanent, as the freshwater and distinct
Mussel assembles its one pink pearl. Time dissolves
But not our memories that harden and crust over,
Becoming agitated with their own sediment. I feel
Uncannily alone with her on this very bleak, wet November
And ready to crack some joke about priests, to release the girl
I always sense is there. We always want to get a laugh
From our mothers, sensing their unspoken problems,
Their laughter restrained by worry. There is such love
In larch and ash, in this tossed woodland grown rough
With winter, its lace of cobwebs across the lower glens
Where light comes through. The sun from above
Is doing its best again. Sun-like warmth, a mother; and tough,
The after-effect of prayer: though memory is enough.

A SCREEN OF LAUREL

I've turned back into the shadowed place where children hide and spy,
The glossy dark of Portugal laurel, the place that in turn may be
A lesser kind of refuge compared to the towering red flags of early

Rhododendron, the one that has found sustenance beyond belief
In a patch of leaf mould, buried deep in the irretrievable boneyard of
Long lost dogs, long forgotten cats and their wild litters and their cry

Late in the night in the chill of early summer. Here in the inner space
Beyond birch and hazel, beyond beech and its great sterile screens,
I have found a place from where I can spy on the great movement of

Ordinance and men, the massive lumbering of armour, the wicked
Arrogance of long-stilled flanges as they are sent battlewards at dawn –
Not again. Not again. This small felt pen I've saved from the house

Now burning, I place it across the little primroses of rescued paper
And write, as quietly as I can, unnoticed by the bleak carriers of war.

THE LONG AGO AT FOTA FRAMEYARD

A boy had died in the war long ago, the one it was
Who took care of that rusty Victorian cistern. Even

The years are leaking now, the years a green scum
That comes to greenish life each spring and thickens

Into the remnant of a greenhouse reservoir. A gloom
Like moonlight still clings to its history. It is as if

The mother who lost him was still in her grey cottage
And a girlfriend waited still by the potting-shed door.

Trapped butterflies thresh themselves to death
In a sudden flurry of sedum and buddleia. You

Would think love had never died in this world, or that
War dispersed itself in a great tank battle that unmade him

So finally. It is as if the Lady of the household
Had merely gone out awhile to prune her muscatels.

SMOKE

in memory of Molly Keane

Reflecting on a half-promise to her I let the cigarette fall;
The cigarette glowing a moment where it fell, its scent
Of something Turkish or faraway, I vividly recall
When I think of the way she turned away and bent
Across the old fender-seat in the darkening billiard-room,
Her shadow stencilled against the bone-white of an Adam fireplace
As she picked up her riding-crop. A house would burn soon
And that would involve both of us: though no release

From our attachments would be in the burnings. A house
Coolly stares back at its father even as it burns, its Russian
Cigarettes falling apart nonchalantly, cool as horses
Sidling impatiently before a stable caves in; a thing set down
Upon a white sofa of snow, this house smoking a vast
Number of cigarettes, one lit from the glow of another,
Window after window. Smoking is hardly a matter of class
At all, but something more nonchalant like your mother

As she boldly plucked a coal from the fire, a lighted coal
To hold at right angles to her lover's Balkan Sobranie
That she had stolen from the silver box beneath the stole
Of white Siberian fur she hoped to place across my knee
That longingly awaited her weight after she'd finished
With the higher world of gentlemen. The house leaned out
Against Irish fields, as indifferent as an unblemished
And beautiful young woman in a kimono who turns about

And drops the cord that holds silk materials together, her
Thought stooping only towards an awkwardly held match.
She has shortened her girths already and awaits the roar
Of hounds coming from the covert, hounds wanting to snatch

At a high scent, their power held at bay in a green holder
Of immense length, their purpose an Egyptian cigarette
She'd promised the MFH. He had been an imperial brigadier
When he took a coffee-cup to her when their eyes first met

But now he is all buttoned up and in full stride
Among hounds heaped like cigarettes on a jackdaw's nest.
The house twists its shoulders away from Ireland in a bid
To avert what comes after the hunt, palpitations in the chest
Of history and stiff drinks for relief. Two separate darts
Of flame will meet to kiss, two to make a seductive move,
And a conflagration of lovers; of Sweet Afton for a start
And two bad people smoking, one still yearning for love.

FULL HOUSE

In these more desolate hours I think of my father
Pushing through alders to catch rainbow trout, making
Hay, as it were, in the sudden swell of a downpour;
Floodwater eddying everywhere, the river alive
With hopes of a harvest without end. Those years
After the War had a kind of emptiness. There were empty
Spaces where people had been, there were mounds
Where houses used to be, depressions for lost gardens
And little clumps of fennel, of survivor geraniums.
I remember picking among shards for something valuable,
Anything that glittered, to lift my father's mind
Off his own depression. It was then they came spilling in,
Old officers who'd survived the long road to Berlin
Or a longer wait in Burma, old men fleeing high taxation
Of the Atlee regime. They are now in my thoughts
As I hold a bottle of rare Madeira with a stained label
And a pepper-mill that I up-end and broadcast
Across this neat row of Carr's water biscuits.
All of this plenitude I prepare for my own company
In this first sunlit day of a real Irish summer.
It is in the deepest possible sense a very warm
Welcome, but for an elegant crowd now long
Gone, gathering by ancient VW and rattling Morris Minor,
At D.H. FitzGerald's house when I was seventeen –
DHF, who was always a little nervous, would
Light the drawing-room fire I'd set weeks earlier
Although it was now a warmed-up May
And I was saturated with sunlight. A fire
Would splutter and spark quietly like a servant
From the earliest days of his childhood. The crowd
Would draw near, as they assemble now in

My imagination, fitfully, from East Cork, from
Tipperary, from Castletownshend and Lismore,
From Ardmore and New Inn. Here is the sliced
Salmon on Barron's toasted brown bread, here
Are the emaciated anchovies and capers; and
Sliced cucumber set like playing cards on a carpet
Of goat's cheese. It's show-and-tell with canapes;
And their noise around his sensational purchase
From Sotheby's or Spink and Son would soon
Be overwhelming, the room as noisy as it is now
In this poem, in this space where I am desolate.

LAMB

Time as buoyant as fresh water in a sunlit shell,
Agitated from elsewhere and the sadness in things
Brittle and autumnal. I turn back along the drenched
Quays and retrace myself in the sand of it, time
That has terrified me with onslaughts of rain.
Another long summer is undone, as consumed and rare
As the rare lamb I ate and chunky Cabernet
We drank together before the weather broke.
Now we are back to the breaking of weather, to
Moss forming again as ferrets and foxes form in
The twistiness of the passing hour; to water
And the habits of water that terrify us.
The un-soaked blood left on my dinner plate
After I'd finished with the warmth of rare lamb
As so much flood-water stained with life, such
Standing water as the waters we journey through:
Sadness of places, and not just circumstance;
Wherever it is that we've found ourselves
When the ache of things break through. I meant
To say the lamb they cooked was beautiful,
Only that time came in a cloudburst while we
Were sitting down, our glasses and our Cabernet;
That time was waiting with its showers of allegory,
Pinching rain for your bare arms, its lamb, its shell.

THEN A CHILD

When they opened the large apricot-coloured door
That seemed bolted such a long time when I was

A child I fell headlong into peach, plum and loquat
Right out of a book I once read concerning

Some other person's childhood. I can't
Remember who it was, but it was a person of substance:

Numb as I am in the face of memoir, glowing
Embers of some other child's excessive fruitfulness

Burned the face of that inner face we've all
Hidden from adults who want us never to claim things

Unearned, or not ours. Why should we have to earn, or be
Bidden forward towards a childhood we might deserve –

Deserved because of parents we didn't choose? Childhood is
Served when a door opens. It's a mirror, but with apricot.

IN UNEXPECTED SNOW

This Lenten hellebore pretending to be a rose
Is so like the year that opened without hope
Only to flourish in a purplish-greenish hue
And dominate all my thoughts on this page

As I retreated from the garden where unexpected
Snow fell with a February fearsomeness. You
Would think that after half a century of weeds
And flowers I'd know not to go disturbing the under-

growth of late winter, but to wait:
So much waiting this year, and last, so much
Of what was postponed or cancelled. The flowers
Here are much further back than they

Should be, even the semi-snowy earth
Has the look of tea preserved and long-forgotten
In a vacuum flask. I pore this dull grey
Liquid of long waiting, I watch the whorl

Of its going down the whirlpool
Of days and days. If the scent in the air
Of this February day is weak with the will
Of unlived beginnings, it's just that

The sun is still not high enough in the sky.
You have to understand the limitations of
Every hellebore, and dress accordingly, to be a rose.
To be a rose, it has to be a dress of the hour.

IN SUNLIGHT

That particular white sand of the secret beach beyond the trees
Is where we find ourselves after a lapse of forty years. When you were

In your twenties and unhappy it was terrible to have sun-burned feet,
The pinching annoyance of sand between hurting toes, the

Hopeless and careless misfortune of it. Now, at your age, even
Distressed razor shells seem less distressing and sharp, their blades

Little more than the sea's tortoise-shell keepsakes. What was
Once menacing is less so in so many ways. There is something else

Entirely in the misfortune of bathing when you are young,
There is so much hope in the settling of blankets on the sand,

In the preparation of towels. At your age you drive grateful toes
Into the sifted earth the sea has made, think only of the luck

You had when you found this cove for both of us, a place far from the city:
The pinkness of rock in full sunlight, a blessed absence of promises.

HEAT

Thirty-five years ago I raced down the red-hot shingle beach
At Agio Roumeli. We had been walking for hours through the Gorge

Of Samaria before we reached the hot Libyan Sea.
                                                    A NATO jet flew

Violently at low altitude as you raced helter-skelter into salt water.

Then, memory: the spectacular clarity of the sea all the way

To Chora Sfakion. A hair-raising ride of Allied evacuation.

The crystal-blue Aegean. An eerie and impoverished silence

Of sixty hair-pin bends. Making love in the stunning heat

Of a Cretan afternoon. We were affectionate and sexually vital:

We were the bravest fighters when roused. And then
                                                    the land itself.

We do fool ourselves into thinking we were happier elsewhere.
Deep down, or, rather, far away, we know damn well we are.

A LOVER OF RARE APPLE VARIETIES

Only recently I discovered that I was the lover of a lover
Of rare apple varieties. It was a thing she'd kept hidden

For years, sometimes the scent was everywhere after
A night of love, fresh linen scented with an unbidden

Feel of apple blossom, unbidden by me but recover-
Ed by her in the way she twisted as if bedclothes were

An orchard in May. Love has that quality, a spring-like blossom
And its great hatred of frost, its yearning for the sun's rays

And the quickening of days. Now I follow her as she roams
From heritage sapling to heritage sapling, my pace

Slower but still firm, the air lightened by all the names
She stores beneath the lattice of her hair and in the small diary

She kept hidden under her pillow. In my innocence
I thought she was keeping a journal about me. What fools

Men are, old poets especially. Now I can plainly see
She was noting the moods of trees, all their compliance

With feeding guides, the annual refinement of RHS rules.
She noted her years of triumph, their prize-winning years,

Misfortunes of intruding deer, thefts of expensive earthenware,
But nothing about my work. When the first frosts lay bare

The limitations of tender bark, when clippings of newspaper
Reviews collapse into a green mould, it will become clear

That my life has been given over to this lover of varieties,
A keeper of Gibson's Russet, Ballinora Pippin. Such trees.

WHITE ALBUM

for Catherine

We settle these heritage sweet-pea into their final resting place
On a balmy evening in early June. From this growing space we hope
They'll rise as 'Black Knight' and 'Mrs Collier' and several other
Unorthodox blossoms; hoping in the way pilgrims anticipate,
Hoping in the way those who have received messages from afar
Hope that the one who set these dried grains into a small
Plug of earth was the One who took promises seriously. As
Serious as you are now, determined, letting hair go grey for
A fresh lifetime of gardening, a new secateurs glinting in your
Wicker trug, a fresh ball of green gardening twine glowing among
Weeds; serious as the expression on your face more than forty
Years ago when you first said you possibly might love me. It
Strikes me as astonishing the way we exchange these names of
Heritage blossoms, two old fuddy-duddies on a June evening,
The way we once exchanged, in a balmy heat whether winter
Or summer, the names of favourite tracks, assessing each other
With 'Savoy Truffle' or 'The Continuing Story of Bungalow Bill.'

THE GREAT WAR

We've almost come now to the edge of the edge of remembering –

When I am gone the precipice begins beyond which
No ear will hear the repeated warnings of an elderly Guardsman
Shell-shocked at the Somme, but standing guard
In old age outside the officers' map-room of Fraher's shop,
Warning me to take cover among the late bundles of the the *Irish Press*
And *The Daily Mail*. Such anxieties will be inaccessible

And the churning of mud will be over. Similarly,
My memories will make way for the brief enfilade of gossip,
The night-time intrusion, the sudden alarm
Of an approaching celebrity columnist. Fresh rivers of blood
Will have a new name, shoulders will heave again
Against the dead-weight of the moment. A comment

May kill us as wars once did. The other war vanishes
In a recessional of named roses; becomes remembrance
Merely, receding into vermilion hybrids
And memory-books of breeders' names. A young man
Passes by talking into his sleeve, conversing with the ether
In the way the wounded did. It is a nightmare,

This renewal. A tank screeching into reverse, a horse backing away.

THE LIFE WITHIN

Cut flowers whose names I've now forgotten don't haunt me
In a conventional way, the way they say things should haunt you

Ever after. The stems, I remember, were rigid and thin
And a strangely weak frail green, the way an elderly
Aristocratic Anglo-Irish lady can be, or a very Waspish professor

Who teaches at an East Coast college. I picked the very long
Unbending stems of a child of a well-born Presbyterian

Elder and for her companions in a mid-afternoon bouquet
I added several common Phlox to be her servants, and ferns

Of course, and half a dozen stems of closely cropped eucalyptus,
With leaves formed into round coppers like buckled coins.

Too much attention turns eucalyptus into bent old pennies,
I thought at once, as I shared the afternoon with a young

Woman florist, a gracious blond youth, Slovak or Hungarian,
Who marvelled at a mature Irishman so fussy with flowers:

'No wrappings?' she marvelled, and marvelling still at the way
I turned what was frail upside-down to keep the life within.

SALVIA RED HUNTSMAN

For thirty odd years flowers had surrounded my wife, waiting patiently,
Making little raids into her heart as when a cutting of a spider-plant

Came from her mother or something wild came from a Co. Kerry aunt
Or cousin. The earliest frost in our marriage took that scarlet tree,

Embothrium, that had come as a pale slip from an Anglo-Irish garden.
Together we destroyed a sensational rosa grandiflora that merely

Wished to flourish above all things on this earth. Too much for us,
At the time, as we were young with the hope of control: to pardon

An excess was beyond our thinking, plants were managed severely
As if they were dogs in training. I thought of all this, our innocent fuss,

The lost hopes of control, as I came back into the house last night
Covered in the wild scent of rampant sage, or a variety of wild sage

With its red huntsman's buttons, plants rampant as hounds in their cage
And my wife laughing at the smell, at the thought of flowers in flight.

PLANTING A WOOD

It didn't begin with us and it won't end even after
We've gone: this impulse to improve upon, this
Colonial settler impulse that's so deep in the heart

Of white folk, we don't even know what's going on.
Take the narrative left in old Mr Buckley's memoirs
Of vast tracts of barren land left idle for planting

North of Mitchelstown, or north of wherever there
Was some other kind of disappeared village. The mounds
Of earth so inconvenient when planting were

Really the unmarked mass graves of a Great Famine,
Boulders needing clearance were the keystones
Of levelled homes. I don't mean to privilege one

Narrative over another, and I don't mean to
Discourage renewal or the best use of cleared land
Or commonage, but trees planted with the best will

In the world were haunted with what lay beneath.
Oaks drove their hard taproots through unforgiving
Layers, the hard pan was broken. Larch and willow,

Austrian fir, it's not a Gaelic song the leaves sang;
But now something more urgent than a nationalist
Feeling compels me to want to begin again. This

Time with human feeling, with a fear that the planet
Entire, with all its historic unhappiness, will disappear.
I pick these acorns that have fallen so early in autumn,

The ones deeply brown or nearly black, and place
Them in a bucket where the sterile ones float. I place
Ten thousand acorns in wet sawdust and watch as

The dead begin to waken. Forty wet zipper bags
Swell with life, ten thousand roots crack through,
And in the long evenings of next spring when each

Oak seedling is four inches tall, we'll walk back
Along all the trails that once made us angry, just
For humanity's sake; just a proper mulch and space.

A VAST CORNER

This bamboo forest I've made for myself has more than
Taken control of any formal plan I might have made for the years

Between the time when I was very young and foolish
Enough to have planted three clumps of arundinaria anceps

In a very restricted city garden and the year just gone
That has caught up with the inevitable way gardens fall

Apart when the first designer has fallen in a great war;
The Great War that took so many gardeners and swept

Out of Ireland in four brief years the memory of what is
Dangerous to plant in restricted spaces and what is wise

To encourage in the capacious margin of a great estate; except
The estates were encumbered the way I am now encumbered,

A much older man, and no longer up to the task that history,
And time passing through chlorophyll, have marked as a task.

DECEMBER ROSE

This frantic rose that wants to bloom so very late into December,
Seems like a petal sent from Atlanta, a pink paper bud

Soon to be washed away in the heavy rain that's due
To fall at any moment from the more bitter north-west;

Though a rose should know its own calendar and what's possible
For a plant in a long enough season. I am more aware than

A pink rose, that's true, of the cold end-of-season breaths
And the absolute shit-hole of growth that the winds can

Make of any season's end. Its knocking on the window-glass
In a force nine gale seems somehow like a diamond-cutter

Trapped in the wrong country. There is such crap in its persistent
Hope, in its nonsense of expectations. The circadian year

Is a command economy, as we all know, and the command
Has come from on high to end such foolishness, such pink paper.

If I owned this rare shrub I wouldn't give in, as I wouldn't give in
    if I had bought that painting in 1974, that dark glossy greeny thing
Of Norah McGuinness. But I was sensible then and very old.
    As old in my head as the artist was when she painted her self-portrait
In pastel. She made herself look dull instead of glamourous,
    Though her eyes betray the glamour of being first-rate. There was
Nothing she could do about that, it just couldn't be hidden. There
    Is probably a Norah McGuinness inside every Irishwoman with pastel
Or brush. But few will get there, as few as the number of camellias
    That survive to blossom fully in June. This unexpectedly luminous
Camellia 'Bob Hope,' it is beyond my pocket at this very moment
    Though next year I might have money enough to splurge.
Its uncanny yellow inside pinkish blossom is a challenge to me,
    A challenge and cheekiness of glossy leaves: forty years, both you
And I have lived with the disappointment of camellias, their huge promise
    of pink buds, the falling away in frosted hopelessness of early May –

Nor would I give in if this perfectly ice-blue Polestar EV
    Were mine to drive while not destroying the planet, a car
That seems as ethereal as the oxygen breathed by clover
    Across a meadow of wild grasses and rattle and sweet
Things that breathe airy life and not death to the planet.
    The handsome young man at the wheel seems equal
To anything as he floats by in blue-tinted glasses. I wonder
    What mother created him to seem as if he'd got all the cream;
The cream of his many unspent years of course, and the
    Other creams that the young may collect without effort. This
Wanting to possess things is becoming something of a
    Bother, it is a lump in my troubled soul, an irritation in the shoe of
The one foot that has always kept me going. Always put one foot
    In front of the other and just keep on going, my mother
Used to say as she looked at the invoices and the high cost of
    Footwear. Is it the mother or the father who sends us

51

On these wild goose chases of quotidian life? I would never give
    In if I could wear that rare and perfect Jaeger Le Coultre
That John Gielgud gave his unfaithful but beautiful Tipperary lover
    Once at a cocktail hour in the Ritz – in nineteen thirty-eight,
Or maybe even closer to the war. Theatres would soon suffer fire,
    Yet plush London would never give in. There is a conflagration
And trouble in our tending to lust after things. It is a yearning
    That could make us starve like Midas. It is effortless like envy
But not that, no, not envy but the yearning to be envied – but
    By whom? Oh, by the objects we ourselves desire. They must
Surely want to be wanted by us, we must be their act of completion
    As the fruit wasp that the flower of the fig tree closes over and
Embalms is a completion of sorts. I want, I want, I want,
    My life says to me in its selfishness. My silver fork is hovering
For a second helping: as Sir John knew when he placed the watch
    On John Perry's faithless wrist, the golden thing is not to give in.

BOARDING AT STANSTED

Thinking how you jumped the queue
In 1944 and hitched a ride on the General's flight

To say goodbye to your aging parents
Before that final crossing of the Rhine.

How surprised they were in the late Stansted sunlight
To see their golden boy

From General Horrocks' staff
When you advanced into their drawing-room,
All limbs intact. I am, I must admit,

Also hoping not to lose a limb
In this shuffling twilight queue, neurasthenic

As a border guard
But happy to have eaten six oysters and quaffed

Too much Asti Spumante. If stars

Appear to be dancing along the Stansted grid
It is not Verey lights above a battlefield

But the lovely navigation light of trade;
Of things coming alive, of such a dizziness as this.

When your last book came over the sea from America
In the month after you'd died it was as if a voice
Had called from afar, or maybe not afar, but from deeper –
Deeper in that diplomatic whirl you understood,

The whirl of carpets and receptions, of men bowing
To each other in a distant country. The gilded formality
Of giving quarter graciously was not now, as it had
Never been, your way of doing business. Rather,
It was a gracious advance, an advance of women,

Of women who knew enough or were lucky in mothers:
Yes, you, matriarchal and dignified. That beautiful binding
and jacket,
The Norton book, I mean, it spoke of an argument settled,
It spoke of sainthood, of J.D. McClatchy and Tobias Wolff,
Of the start and finish of legends, of Ireland's azurite vowels.

It was magnificent how you could unpick the heavy lock
In the side-gate of history, the one camouflaged by wet
Laurel leaves where a woman in a trench-coat might wait
For her moment. How does one begin, as Lois wonders

In that novel by Elizabeth Bowen; how does a lover
Remain faithful in unfinished revolutions? To write
In the light of what will be, where hope becomes law,
That was your one long journey. Where a young mother
Was disturbed in her night-feed, moving to the night-lit

Window, pen and child in hand, an aeon opened.
Reading these poems to my daughter as we catch
The early Luas in Rialto, sunlight on Guinness cottages,
Something youthful of you illuminates our day: the light in
That voice of you from far away, your pen behind a curtain.

FROM SALONICA

The bulky Famine ship that came over the sea was a fork

And never a spoon: the sea couldn't be bothered.
The shore was a surprise of place-settings
Neatly arranged, the moist food ample

And nourishing, the Ajax sailing for Bristol,
Sixty boxes of salmon, three hundred lambs aboard.
Inbound, the Iona from Philadelphia,
Wanting to be part of our story, a berth in the pageant

That would go on and on. Sugar from Trinidad

For our betters in the city, the Kaffirland
With guano, the Aurora with Bangor manure.
The Lizzie Anne for Alexandria, Seagull from Odessa;

And from Salonica, the Flying Cloud.
Something miraculous in the continuity of trade,
As miraculous as the way we're still upset
With deaths in unmarked famine graves. But what

Was a Captain to do, or a shipping agent,

When the unchartered died beneath their wake?
Such plenty as the sea has, such a plenitude of trade,
Is only in the keeping going between a chosen few,

The chosen who come aboard this ship of a poem,
Its cargo discharged, it lyric intent;
Aboard as a chandler at high tide on the South jetty,
Rum in his full decanter. His laden bulk, his behemoth.

EARLY EVENING AT BALLYFERRITER

Wild screams from two Irish Language classes
As they enter the cold sea, a sea now
Of unsteady adolescent colours, a great chorus
Of disturbed sea-water One brave

Boy-grammarian splashes the others
And dives into the protective deep.
I turn and fix my gaze on the far shore,
Waiting, like the patient violinist

Giuliano Carmignola, in Locatelli's
Concerto No.10 for violin, strings and continuo,
Waiting for the returning wave of salt
That crashes orchestral upon the swimmers,

But see, instead, the conductor's flash
Of a gannet as it wheels and dives with metallic fire;
And a boy, bayonet and baton, splitting open
The vast summer we share. And its arrangement.

CITIES OF ROMANIA

for Eiléan Ní Chuilleanáin

I.   CONSTANTA

This dusty black cat guarding the Casino at Constanta
Looks at me with the penetrating, stark eyes
Of a Belle Epoque border guard. She guards
Her breakfast hour with all the assertion of
Her lost countess. Such eyes when they meet mine
Are as implacable as the Black Sea, as deep
As water compressed between two regimes.
There is Sauterne soaked into this sunlit yellow,
Something of the anxious luxury of Europe lives on
In the hour. When time passes croupiers have claws.
A north wind ruffles her coat, and a breakwater
Of concrete pawns that never worked in August 1914
Consoles us now with its austere way, the way
It leans into the morning mist. If you listen carefully,
Listen patient as a black cat in a casino, you can hear
The Bucharest-Paris Express, hiss of flanged wheels.

II.   BUCHAREST

Here France is the drip-feed that sustains a heart –
I walk with Bucharest's best librarian, Roland Barthes,
Who tells me how difficult it is to square the circle
Of Europe. France has been in situ since the patriot died;
And a rich network of streets between this glazing of
Radisson-Bleu and Banc National de Paris is carved
From a fretwork that could only be French. The streets
Of Bucharest forever look Westward, this paradise
Of cut stone could be Avenue Mac-Mahon or Ave de Ternes

But I digress, and with all the prejudice of the West –
And this waiter who carefully up-ends a tiki-glass
Into a bed of ice, edging towards a crystalized Manhattan,
Is the best symbol yet of all artistry in a state of flux:
As Europe is upended, or as the patriotic young always are.

III.   CRAIOVA

After such vast Danubian wheat-fields, this German crane
Delays us with its heavy duty of penetrating, gigantic teeth
Lodged in the spleen of a Ceausescu-era apartment block.
Water bleeds from shattered bathrooms, a blood-letting
On the road ahead. Impatient and red, a Maserati
Screams past through the narrow gap; such testosterone
Unwilling to wait. As we wait, and calmly, for the road
To clear. Something about transformation, but in
A waiting land. The city is perplexed with promise.
Its young, who must be the young of regional powers
Or the offspring of settled commerce, sit upright
And eager to learn the merest small thing. They have heard
What the old know nothing about: history settling back again
After a great trauma, Romania facing into a morning light.

Our lives have compressed darkly
Into this one frozen spot. The cry of the wireless it is, and the one

Familiar voice of a broadcast. Oh God,
Let no invader take this speaker from his microphone,
We are cowering below his words in our fragile house.
Smoke is no armour, nor is it

A rock. My mother is still nursing the wounded
Who can hardly breath, there is such grief in Templemeads;
And the Irish Guards are gone beyond the Arctic line.
Wary as a horse, my brother has slipped outside.

Will there be an ugly end to him? The vibrations of a night train
Knock this Yearbook from the oil cloth

Where my father left it. I read
In the half-light and the quiet of dreams before war came:
There was a Mediterranean in their love-making
Before he was called to arms. The way she urges him to write

Is their way of staying alive; and this book, with its war addresses
Marked in red, seems crushed and frail as a bleeding lung.

IN MEMORY OF SERGEI ALEXANDROVICH YESENIN

History in our wet country had exited to the right, leaving us
With the most unfortunate prospects. It was not the fault
Of anyone in particular, I think, or even of any class of persons
Among the living or the dead. I do remember being young and
Comforted by communism or communism's stark reading of
The sum of experiences a working-class child might have had
When inexorably trapped at a sub working-class fireside.
The fire spluttered with the wet, stolen timber I'd shouldered
Like a soldier disembarking at Corunna or Gallipoli, a soldier
Or a soldier's son with the weight of want on his wet shoulders.
It is important to have a wide view of history when you have
Nothing else. I was far from plenty but not alarmed. I was, I knew,
Much stronger than my father could ever be. Yet of his blood,
Of that last vast proletariat stumbling ahead without the hope
From history. Panic seemed to grip the adult, but not his child.
How strange that is. Yet how comforting it was, not to be
The kind of child who panics. I would meet the knife that history
Flung at me with an unflinching child's stare. Where it lodged
In the damp plaster above my left eye was a date I had scratched
In confidence. I can't remember the year, but I can recall
The immense confidence in my destitute self as I nicked
A date in the pink distemper above my mother's bed. She
Was the warmth and the comfort. It was her and me against
All the forces of history that seemed to so distress my
Family. It must have been the forces of life against the great force
Of history that troubles fathers. We were detritus, socially
Unneeded, an excess of poor that only the requirements
Of a war economy could make relevant and useful. We were,
To be absolutely blunt, great unwashed fools of history,
As inert as our country, as frail as its superstitions. Where was
The Elysium that Ireland dreamed of, where was the God

That history promised? Freedom requires property or land,
Or both, so that the bourgeoisie can be sentimental, print
Poems in praise of themselves, or print some other form
Of conveyance: have a country to covet and hoard, a nation –
But I digress. I digress from that point in the life of a child
Where political calls to action have no meaning, where a
Voice raised in the interest of the working poor sounds
Hollow and wretched when heard through the broken
Window-panes of a labourer's cottage. History is the gold
Hoard that giveth and giveth. Here, let me polish this
Ingot that distressed Yesenin handed to me through this broken
Window: how heavy it is in the hands of a child; and how
Pitiful that it must be passed back to some Bolshevik
Passing beneath the window, some professional
Whore-monger of a son just out of post-graduate school
And in search of a career. Let's hide this ingot, Yesenin,
Out of sheer black-guarding and working-class unreliability
In the face of history, let's not empower anyone to speak
On our behalf. Let us hoard for ourselves the suffering:
So chthonic it cannot become words in the mouths
Of persons not born poor. Though hope in a child is unbearably
Brilliant. It is gold. And in its metallic phase it glows
And changes. It becomes worlds, this suffering; it
Outshines every one of its possible meanings. It leaves
A trail of plenty in its wake. It names every single child
That ever had a frightened father, it names and raises
The dead in every unmarked grave in Europe. It stands
In defiance. It is unafraid in the face of so much pain,
This ingot of gold that childhood bequeaths, this ounce
Worth a thousand that we have hidden in a woodpile
From Cossacks and Bolsheviks. I have been looking forward
For half a century, Yesenin. You, you've been not
At peace with yourself for twice as long as that. Not

At peace in the way poets should always ultimately
Promise peace to the page. Sergei Alexandrovich Yesenin,
It is so typical of you to write that last poem of yours
In your own blood; typical, I mean, of the tendency
For self-harm among the destitute poor. A calculating
Bourgeois would have used someone else's blood, but
You, like the Irish poor I knew as a child, would self-mutilate
To tell the truth. This is not the road to plenty. This,
Dear Sergei, is not the highest pathway in the road
Of gold. Not the experience, not the plenty we remember.

IN OLD SHANGHAI

This impeccable row of roundly potted Chinese bamboo
Has caught us unawares on an evening in Shanghai.
Just when we thought our lives had been, up to now,
Something that only happened between us. I can see why

It is the world that has tried every which way to find
A moon-gate by which it might enter the spaces we made
Since the day we met; though it is bamboo that travels blind,
Edging across the weak pattern before all calligraphy fails

In a series of inky splatters. It is better to begin in lust
As a night in China does, lustily feeding shoppers into
The crowded Nanjing Road, full of yuan and trust,
Full of red and gold. If bamboos keep breaking through

To index every neon light it is only because the Twenties
Are upon us again and all the women seem thin in a thin
New light, their young men adorable in black silk clothes.
This is Shanghai and the world is young, and this pattern

Of layering everything into the heavy lacquer of a poem
Becomes young again in the paperwork of girl and boy –
Though we are far away we were never more at home
Than in this capital of moonlit stone, fine bamboo, red chai.

A TRUE ORIGINAL

It was at your Bar Mitzvah in old Cork city
In the very long ago when everyone was so happy
That Lord Mayor Goldberg gave you that silver gift
Of a Parker 75, though there was no clip

Set into the tassie, which according to Lih-Tah Wong's
Handbook means that it was not a true original.
It was 'The Banks of My Own Lovely Lee' they sang in Hebrew
And all sang it because everyone was then so happy

To be young and full of beginnings and medical degrees.
A farming uncle had sent a straw box of almonds
So that we might never forget, not even in Cork,
Where a concert could delay us on the way to a Promised

Land. The Rosenberg String Band played on and on, but
'Something's happened to old Ireland,' Mayor Goldberg said,
'a land once as lovely as a Swan 34,' and moved at a clip
Out of Irish public life. It was at your Bar Mitzvah.

BELLS

I am with old professors, Seán Lucy and Seán O Tuama,

In a tiny car-park of Cork City Library. It must be
Long ago, the way we are together in this heavy,
Drenching rain after a July seminar on Yeats.
Something has just occurred in our understanding
Of what it means to be still alive. This car-park,
Which is really only a builders' yard left behind
In Nineteen Seventy Eight after an urgent renovation
Of the Library staff-room, this dank yard
Is beginning to flood as sheets of water
Slip greasily from the sky. Right now we are all
Soaked to the skin like the still alive; it is as if
Dying and losing the best kind of people was only
A dream that passes quickly. As we lean-in together
To what's left of a bicycle-shed we listen to the rain's
Ferocious clamour. Ag clagarnach, Seán O Tuama says,
One of the precise Irish words for this kind of rain.
Does that come from the word for 'bell' in the Irish,
Seán Lucy asks, you know 'an clog,' that bell-sound.
No, more like a boot, a jack-boot on the roof of language,

Though this rain is belling down in cathedrals of sound.

A FOX IN THE WHINS

March's ugly violence and circadian wickedness
Lifts these platted hems of the willow's dress

And shames the sunlight that must surely arrive
As crowds from Cheltenham come home to live

Their lives more ordinary and less filled with chance.
The frosted forsythia and mimosa's obedience

Is the catechism of seasons: a woman chitting potatoes
In a far potting shed, those early Spring floods

Making temporary lakes beneath the house,
Cobalt blue of late winter water, resting grouse

Far from the nearest guns. Two strange dogs,
one Chihuahua, the other Shipperke, ease out of the bog

And unwind, snake-like, beneath my feet,
One moves on when it sees I can do nothing for it

And slips right back into the first page of a novel
By Mrs. Molly Keane, that page where things are brutal

Between primrose and watercress. Wind tightens
The sly grip of this season by a notch, one fox in the whins

Howls for a chase. A memory of words drives me back
Indoors, to settle these dogs beneath glass and shellac.

DEER IN THE BIRCHES

Disturbances in the sunlit corridors and laughter
Of the young as they think of anywhere other than here,
Their end of semester excitement trembles in the water
In my water-glass. Hardly anything could be as clear

As the cocksure happiness of Seniors finally getting away –
That young man with his A+ essay on Louis MacNeice,
His girlfriend who cracked the complexity and interplay
Of musical allusions in Derek Mahon, they blow kiss

After kiss through my open door. They are insane
And light-hearted with ideas of Europe. I am in no hurry
As I turn to look through the tall windows of Old Main,
Anaesthetized by a memory of home. Smells of blueberry

Scones and strong coffee penetrate though the air-
conditioning while I stand and see through a heat haze
The liquid patterns of a deer in the birches. It stares
At this campus commotion of human kind, it delays

Just a moment before turning as its ancestors did
At the end of those College semesters, before so many wars
When the young fled outward and suddenly died
In places they had never read about. A deer twitches its ears

As animals do when taking something in. It ruminates
Upon more than grass and sapling bark
Before it clears without effort the high College gates,
Sure of meaning at the end of things, secure in its dark.

REMEMBERING THE GREAT FAMINE

I love the way we've appropriated the precise
And particular suffering of the destitute poor –
This company director, a man no doubt sincere
And full of after-dinner goodwill, tells the first lies

Of this evening, saying how he needs to be
True to the suffering of his ancestors; and this
Chartered Accountant talks of his real distress
When he thinks of the same suffering. He

Says he wants to go down on his knees to pray,
Sometimes, when he thinks of his people
Falling by the West Cork wayside. Respectable
Persons in the best dinner-jackets pay

Such homage, and yet, I know, these two,
However slightly drunk and however wholly kind,
Have got their origins in a twist. I have a good mind
To recall their ancestors, to name the retinue

Of cattle dealers and high grade salt merchants
From whence they came. But I let bygones
Be bygones, even if my poems won't. My poems
Keep digging up the facts; how at the entrance

To Cork harbour, that late summer of Black '47,
A ship carrying tons of mutton, beef and pork
Departed for the London trade; how in the dark
The destitute were about what is market-driven

About Ireland, and how immoral our meat-trade.
We watched our own die so that our burgeois prospered.
Prosperity was only as good as how much the poor could bear –
What the poor suffered should be left to themselves instead.

FEROCIOUS RAIN

I sing in the heavy autumn rain, I fold a weak umbrella
And take the freshened sting, needles of Friday's water

Against my face. The weather's rough hair brushes
Against me, the sheer tumult of it, the beast
Lashing against skin, too heavy to argue.

I tell myself that this must be what happens
When the years unfold above you, a miasma of time

So casually indifferent and disruptive. The answers
Bounce off the pavement, no good in these upright nails:

A blue thing and a bleak thing is rain, as metallic as hinges.
The years before and the years ahead of me are swinging

Like gates swinging in a persistent storm; and in the gap
This heavier rain. Singing in such rain was always daft

Unless you were very good-looking and young. I was
Young, at least, before the gates opened in a sudden gust,

A zephyr like the San Francisco Zephyr I arrived upon
When time crossed the Humboldt River and the Forty

Mile Desert and we came into an area of Pinot Noir
Where mindfulness was on a label, a sunlit mindfulness

That closed quickly around me as I searched for the bus-
Depot and its shelter that might take me elsewhere; as you,

Dear passenger, have been taken to a drier place by my poem,
Our mutual past cold as Amtrak Zephyrs shunting in heavy rain.

BLOOMSDAY, SANDYCOVE, 2022

I only came here for the coddle and hard dry bread,
But this crowd has swept me along into the froth
Of 1904, the band playing as if on a promenade
And straw boaters floating on the print of sunlight

Like sycamore wings. The L.E. James Joyce on site
And incongruous as Trieste, though all my thoughts
Are of boats and children and ponds. White
As our pale hands, homes are glued to the spot

Where money still resides. Where Jesuits fought
With their consciences, the children of privilege
Will be-sport themselves still, taking for excuse

A book and not 'Throwaway' in the Cup at Ascot.
It is like somebody brought a winner into the village:

The day a golden rosette, his book such good news.

THE NATIVE LANGUAGE

With effort I'm trying to leap back to language lessons of youth,
An honest effort to make sense of what's in history. Scholars
At my evening talk don't feel any empathy with the Irish Loyalist

Experience so that I must eschew revisionism, share insights
From the best words in our native language. I shall give them trees

First of all: how learóg/larch, fearnóg/alder, fuinseog/ash were rent
From the flourishing earth, and even an sáileach sa saileán

Or sally in the sally grove, was not left undisturbed but
Fenced in as ceantar camhnaithe géim or game reserve. Only

Colonists didn't take to the woods like our ancestors, except on days
In search of an piasún/ the pheasant and an creabhar/woodcock.

It's funny how land preserved meant land excluded, except for
The few, the planters. Níor thug siad sa choill orthu féin, these

Williamites and the Huguenots who came with the first wave. No,
They didn't take themselves to the woods like us, no; except

To speak to the dóiteóirí gualaigh/ charcoal burners of the Cúl
Na Smutáin, that backward place of burning embers beyond

Each great demesne. Trees became ordinance, ploughs and swords to
Defend Na Péindlithe/ Penal Laws. Tonight I need to speak softly to this

New class of bourgeois native persons, language enthusiasts of the Gael,
Who now wish to hear of luxury interiors in the fiction of Elizabeth

Bowen or of the small toy dogs wrapped in Burberry scarves in the fiction
Of Mrs Molly Keane. And of how, as the greatest houses burned,

Coimeád siad a gcuid fuaraigeantacht i rith an sceimhlitheoireacht –
That's it, how they kept a cool head during nights of native terror.

A DEMESNE OF FLOWERS

*'Be thou faithful unto death, and I will give thee
A crown of life.'* – Revelations XI

I take in these flower arrangements at Carrowdore:
It is a ridiculous hope and no obligation
Of mine to catalogue flowers made of Louis MacNeice poems.
It is that very thing that is fatally attractive
In a small enclave, of above average height,
That hovers subtly over cut flowers and cut stones.
Here, I peel away the lacquer, fretwork and inlay
Of a not insignificant people, to reveal a fury
Of enterprise, something that has both
A distinctive style and the wherewithal to praise God.
Because of these cut flowers I now lift the lid
On a different assembly, and, arriving in Cork,
See that it is the South's particular sensibilities I note
In the arrangement of history; in things that set us apart.
As there are Gallweys and Lawtons to trade
So there are others who merely look on and marvel
At the wealth of ladies, the La Touche banknotes,
The very Art of Italy that folds into a Penrose.
It is Mr. Burchell lighting the last boiler at Bandon Co-Op
Before setting off to England to fight a great war;
It is the Swanson sisters, leaving Douglas Village
On their two manly motor-bikes, heading for Ballykinlar Camp;
It is a West Cork farmer covering a bridge in Pothus Wood.
It is my ridiculous hope to get inside that frame
Now only strong enough to hold a burden of flowers.
With this hurling-stick of a pen I could break glass
And disturb the settling peace of things. Here, I place
Those elements of Irish life in my green pipette
And shake and shake. Though I hear nothing

Shattering, I can hear the creak of a bamboo chair
As it settles in a book by Elizabeth Bowen,
I can hear the clink of a glass in Molly Keane, the sharp
Edge created by an attractive rival: the sound of horses
Cantering over winter ice, here, beneath elms on the back-avenue,
And a more ordinary Protestant life as it angles away
On a bike, a High Nelly that Miss Cliffe used
To spend her summer mornings in Dungarvan –
Miss Cliffe who kept to the edge of William Trevor's
Prose, whose world was old ledgers and glass jars:
Though it is always October, leafy Lismore weather,
That she cycles into, mostly leaf-mould, remembrance.
Carrowdore, then, and that most select vestry of Ulster –
Though across the yard, almost overlooked, the work
Of Carrowdore women, the sheer pluck of flower-arrangement
In the face of a bombing campaign; how when we have
No business with techniques of verse, and no license,
We can still make sense with a florist's best stock.
There is hardly more than trimmed euphorbia between the poem
And the poet: that, dear Bishop MacNeice, was their message
To your bright BBC son. Wild fuchsia
May cover his grave, but the world is as the son ordained,
A billowing snowfall of gypsophila florets, carefully framed.

PIEDMONT

i.m. James Simmons

Yet more imperfect blue sonnets around

Every corner, a hand-dying of bleached linen:
These Piedmontese dream awkward dreams;
Which is why I am so grateful, Jimmy,

To have heard your heart-felt songs of different
Victims, these strangers of the Northern
Line who fell beyond the borders where

Our hearing could not reach. Plain speech
And delicate thread, a feel for the loom,
You sang of linen workers dead in a ditch,

Names like Montgomery, Romily and Stone,
And all the local griefs that never came
Within hearing range of our quiet Rome.

Thank you for bringing me to Piedmont,
A kind of Ulster province north of the Vatican;
Lovely to see so fully reformed a life

In full swing among apple groves and vines,
Yet still in constant touch with pilgrims
Of the far Ardense. History was real to you,

As familial as the chords of a dance-band
In festive Turino. It was such a joy to meet
Signor Hewitt, a joy to be introduced

To the paterfamilias over a grappa or two;
To see his kin working still the permanent
Way between North Down, Asti and Bra.

Though she couldn't go in, being a woman.
In those days only waitresses were allowed,
Easing in the side doors to kitchens and towels,
While the men, Yeats and his friends,
Stood forlornly on the privileged threshold,
Thinking of a place more suitable for a
Woman. Claridges, then, its lounge piano
playing and tilted snipes of champagne,
Though the woman brought urgent requests
And political questions. Ernst Toller and
Ethel driven to tears by Yeats' indifference,
His haughty Irishness. No, he would not
Nominate a man in prison; no he would not
Speak of things European. He was, at that
Moment, closing against the world, regretting
His name on a petition for Casement. What
Made Toller and Ethel cry was the thought
Of Carl von Ossietsky in a Hitler jail and
The saving wreath of a Nobel. No friend
Of any hero not Irish, Yeats was firm in thought,
And von Ossietsky dead in a Nazi onslaught.

BECOMING CECIL HURWITZ

Two large manila envelopes with nothing more
Important than an obituary of Lord Gowrie

And the inaudible noise from a Jazz brochure,
The furious playing of the first public events

After pandemic. The people have had
A heart transplant and I hope they keep going:

Shop windows reassert themselves, trinkets
And silver-bells are the Christmas battle-cries

And it's all to play for once again.
I think of your love of heavy brown envelopes, Cecil,

And how they contained instructions and prayers.
I can see that I've slowly become you

In these years of shutdown and disease,
Walking as I am in the apocalypse

You predicted so very long ago.
Funny how we become part of a city by merely

Being there. Our walking creates an architecture,
Our memories become so much frieze and cornice.

I see the whole of history in the merest small window –
October, lights coming on in Goldberg's pub.

READING SHOLOM ALEICHEM

These reflections of hollow, pointed river-reeds in the water
Give this day a space as wide as God. And when you

Grow older, as old as I am now writing these words
Beneath the awning of Goldberg's pub, you see,

Stretching all the way down Albert Road, beyond
The emptiness of the Passage West railway terminus,

That the world is suddenly crowded with the young:
That's what it really means, to be old; as old

As Cecil Hurwitz bustling through Cork city each day,
Rushing to end things before noon because, he said,

A city in the afternoon belongs to the young – and, anyway,
Early morning always belonged to the old. It is not

That we survive our own years but that the new world
Beyond these reeds swaying in my head is a breathless crush

Of the young. I can hear them approaching from beyond
As I wait for a single berth I booked earlier. That Dnipro ferry.

MARIA JOAO PIRES ON A SEPTEMBER EVENING

Whose fingers have rushed into the house like so many
Field mice and now race up and down the ivories
That were so still all summer long. They play, they tumble
Miraculously from thimble to thimble, all andante
With the wheaten dust of Mozart, Allegro with Amadeus,
Fitful as all of Austria in a tizzy. Somewhere the absolutely
Straight lines of sanity have gone, the chaff of the field
Is fallen on her arresting pedals. If this Sonata could only
Hold its nerve; No. 17, its tickled Allegretto, its vulnerable
Raised arms disturbed by the tails of playing mice. All
Of her, the spite of autumn. Piano upright. The end of it.

AN EXILED WRITER

for Peter Nazareth

Let's be mindful that we feel at home in two countries
And live in the one as if the other didn't exist,

Though the other keeps nagging like a second childhood.
A country knocks at the door, wanting more food,

The way an orphan might implore us. Each refugee
Flees from a country that keeps following, a country

That doesn't want to go home. Here we are,
On an indifferent verandah without visible scars:

Our first country keeps banging on the stained glass
Window, the one erected in honour of peace,

While we cower at the table farthest from the door.
In here suffering is meaningful and our dinner

Is mindful of the burdens outside. Here, food
Is assertive but gives no offence. Waiters are shrewd

In this second country, they invite us to reframe
Our pain; to inhabit just one island nation

Where the ways are kind and the myths are mindful –
Where the voices above dinner plates are alert and reciprocal.

ELEGY BETWEEN WORLDS

in memory of Micheál O Súilleabháin

I.   IDIR EATARTHU

At the turning of the road, a piano, a goldcrest,
A golden bird that finds the bass notes to begin
At the heart of a life that had depths. Three shafts
Of death disturb us, as death cannot be governed
By our prepositions; nor can its wings signify

Possession in the way Micheál was possessive.
The wine-glass of one life is emptied now, but still
Songs come up out of the wind like the ghost
Of a hedge-school near Clonmel. There is no end
To the knowledge he left on these ivories; even

These wet hedge-rows whistle his name
And music he possessed possesses us still.
The vibrations left behind in the frame,
The tremble and variations, they assert again
The movement of his eye, his hands' assertion.

II.   HEARTWORK

At the racing heart of Heartwork is a musical fox
Fabulously escaping: no piper shall have him
At the end of his piping, none but the scales
That protect living things. The metrical forms
Have a wildness within. Or such passions as
You knew, Micheál, when the hunt was in you
Between isle and marsh, piano and bodhrán.

III. TEMPLUM

The high curling notes and the notes in restraint
Rise and fall between such veils of sound
As part in that space where a piano is found,
As part in the space where you played. Such saints
Of the Gael where you were a prince are a comfort
In this terrible era. Micheál, you were the scribe
With a keyboard for pen, and a soul transcribed
Into celestial notations. And there too, without effort,

A great procession of gifted women, Fanny Power,
Lady Maisterton, attend to you in the fading hour,
Telling you yet again of collectors of music, of
The soul of all Ireland that folded into you.
Scholar-soloist, maestro from Clonmel, it's true
Skylarks rose when you played. The skies moved.

HARP MUSIC

I.   A FEW PREPARED REMARKS ON ALICE COLTRANE

That she studied Detroit in Paris with Bill Powell
And conquered all, including men of music –
Which was a kind of miracle before ashrams
Would deliver their own kinds of miracle.

Go down those stairs and talk to Thelonious Monk,

Joe Hunt and Chick Correa: it was how
Alice grew out of Paris and into John.

Vedantic chants, Christian hymns,
Four little kids, widowed mother, twelve albums:
You would think one human heart could hardly hold such weight.

Hers was the small bird of the soul
                    Flitting in the saffron of Radhe-Shya

II.   SOME PRELIMINARY NOTES ON DOROTHY ASHBY

This is not the harp that once in Tara's halls.

There was a small African hotel in the great harp's frame
Before 'Moonlight in Vermont' and 'Charmaine.'

In 'Pawky' the tightened string rises and rises
As if a string could escape through a flute.
How can a string be a wind instrument and not
Be damaged? There is that kind of freedom in music,
A freedom of incremental chains, lustrous, harp-like.

There really is harp freedom, gold-plated.

If you've got privilege you can never truly understand this:
You need to have been imprisoned for carrying a harp.

III.   IMPROMPTU NOTES ON TRIONA MARSHALL

So crowded out by men in our Gaelic male-strum
That the 'March of the King of Laois' seems a religious retreat
In a deep ashram of only-women.

Those left behind on the quaysides of 1603 and 1691
Find in you an abandoned harp. How you fight

For your space in the fast frigate of 'Planxty McGowans,'
Rising above the foam,

Immortal in music, unassailably feminine.

Oh! Come back with me to 'O'Carolan's Farewell,'
To 'Carraroe' and its golden ring.

When God made music he made plenty;
He made a plenitude in the parish of strong women.

OPERA CAKE AT COCOA CAFE

Things I had hungered for at the beginning of this year
Are as unchanged as this chic, neat café that serves

Lattes and flat whites and long chocolate slices
Called 'opera cakes.' As I live in a city without opera
I can't ignore the indulgence of my taking two slices

Just for my own self, as I took two slices and not one
The very minute I was born and not a moment later.

This instinct for excess inside me, this year that is
Neither good nor bad but ready to be sliced by me

For my own childish benefit, it is like a decision made
In a new intake of breath, in a poem by a higher power.

CHANGING PLANES AT NEWARK

After this oceanic struggle on the crowded concourse
I let go of air rage and begin to sing

Above my full NY breakfast and water with ice.
I've been upgraded to First Class –

Because of my no particular hurry.
I gave way to a man with expensive bags, to a man of worry,

His tale of lost connections and a business deal
In jeopardy. How could I also not feel

The force of human empathy:
This is the American life, a Newark quandary

At seven-thirty am –
Though not in the selling business I can feel the pain

Of turning up too late with an idea,
Of just reaching a conference room cleared

Of those who might have bought into
My one brilliant pitch that flew from Chicago

Overnight. I may have landed just too late
As well, the poem inside me missing its distant gate,

To sit here as resolute as old Norman MacCaig,
Diminished as a small bairn in a basking-shark's wake.

IN OLD NEW YORK

I.   WEST 79TH AND RIVERSIDE DRIVE

There was something between us
From our own written-down lives.
Maybe it was a changing street light
Or lights arranged for Hannukah
That illuminated our time within –
A mirage of moving traffic, a film
Edited without sound, a fuss of chrome;
An unhappy barman who wouldn't
Serve food at a time when any boy
Might hunger for something. If there
Was it was only because of a thing
In Louis MacNeice, a strong yearning
Never to leave but having to leave
On that ship easing away to the war.
Don't go, the Hannukah lights cried,
Turn to look at us. It's only Eleanor.

II.   DISCUSSING CLAIRE KEEGAN ON WEST 64TH

Pausing for a moment while three fire-engines pass,
I notice a shower of *Post-It* notes settling on the window-sill.
A writer's bulky file of thoughts has fallen from the seventh floor
In an aurora of butterflies. One yellow moment jostles another.

Did you notice the measured space between each fire-engine
And its urgent follower? As if crisis had a pattern somehow.
We should continue but we pause. A child may have to wear
A dead child's clothes before this quiet conversation ends.

III. A LIGHT SNOW ON WEST 66TH

I walked down Amsterdam to W66th and Juilliard School
When a light snow fell early, too early in its audition
For a lead part in winter. Traffic drew curtains on its indecision
And the artistes withdrew. New York is no fool
When it comes to the seasons. Fall hadn't quite finished
Its recitation of leaves; there were late actors blowing
Shapes in the breeze, and a tree-violinist still bowing
Madly as at a September concert. A boy from the Tisch

Was re-writing the script in a frantic manner. I tried not
To interfere in the way a poet always wants to interfere,
Creating enjambment, wanting it to snow in two lines
Or fewer. Being Irish I had little experience of distraught
Consequences in early snow. The *Pogues* were in my ear
From a funeral in Nenagh. Let it go, Shane said, let it snow.

IV. A MIGRATION OF SOULS

I need to stop remembering, to have this poem end
At the junction of Eight Avenue and West 72nd.
Where I had lingered as a very young man more
Than forty years ago. We were innocent and stunned,
Ridiculous new arrival and serious academic friends,
As we watched Yoko march across grief's corridor

To teach us, somehow, of her deep migrating soul.
Today in Strawberry Fields, a designated quiet zone,
I listen to a youth, my age then, and his iPhone
As they create voice and accompaniment. His full,
Lush notes penetrate the air in a cascade of tones,
Banishing all impediment and signs. Even stones,

Stone and ashlar, of Congregation Shearith Israel,
Curtsy in homage. See, there's something the young
Know for certain that the elderly have now lost. I bring
Seven votive candles, an Irish Catholic's catalogue
Of grief, make to light my sanctuary lamps, but swing
Away in hesitation. The young here must feel something

I could never second-guess. I place my candles
Back in the past where they belong. They should stay
Back home where I keep those perfections of memory.
They should burn in the privacy of a worn LP. We mishandle
Each moment like the LP sleeve. This decade's intense privacy
Is something else again, shooing communal folk away

And barring the garrulous gesture. I am too old
To reimagine the old, I cannot conform myself to this
Age, like the ancients in Romans 1:2. The young may kiss
Every shrine they wish, but I'm beyond that fold
Wandering the streets with seven small candles
And this poem ending at a junction, or some such place.

V.   AT ST PATRICK'S CATHEDRAL

Did William Rudolph O'Donovan light candles here –
Candles for a true likeness of Winslow Homer
In bronze? Or the younger Maurice Brazil Prendergast
As he struggled with the new way of looking at a beach
In oils? Such American subtleties that the immigrant
Irish might have missed. Though not the music, not
That, nor the soul wholly given away to candles glowing
In a great vault and the echoes, mysteriously, of
Atlantic migrations of two million souls or more, souls
Assembling penny by penny, as they are now in this
Procession of the faithful, of the never going to return.

VI.   BUYING AN ELIZABETH BISHOP ON COLUMBUS AVE.

You really only need a Dolmetsch clavicord
And a constipated kitten to be attached
To this world, and attached for good
And all…………… 'My first customer of today,'
The old hippie surprises me with speech
And I reply: 'From three thousand miles,
Back where the fish are large, the sky pistachio.'

And he asked me if I'd ever been to Listouch
Or the Gap of Dunhoe, or Caskel or Cujden
On the Galway coast. And I confirm –
To all those places, and more, as Elizabeth was
Back in '37; with a coal fire burning in Benner's Hotel
And many suppers of soup and cheese. On West 70th
The sky lit up with lies. My sly deed was done.

VII.   HE HAS ENOUGH WATER

Here on W79th I am speaking to a kidnapped Israeli.
It is a secret miracle, but of the kind I always believe in:
He says I sound like Isaac Bachevis Singer above the din
Of a Coney Island diner and he laughs when he
Hears that I am an Irishman on an old Blackberry
That I hid in a ditch when I was kidnapped by the IRA.
We are both hiding in tunnels with nothing left to say
To the surface where history fell out of sympathy

With his nation and mine. He has enough water
And I have enough wine. His *Keyone* to my *Aurora*
Is crystal clear. A miracle. A miracle. It is like a poem –
The poetry of encryption on a silicon wafer,
Or someone Jewish who walked on the Sea at Galilee,
Walking on waters of love, calling still on a phone.

VIII. IN OLD NEW YORK

I would like to thank a mysterious Foundation that placed me
Here on the satin pillows of this expensive hotel. All based
Upon a misunderstanding, I should explain, that arose

When I put both the ingredients for Old Fashioned and the place-
Settings for a formal dinner as advised by the head waiter
Of this establishment into a very modest rhyming poem.

As things stand in Ireland, I can't apologise for rhyming well;
Not when we're so very far away from St Patrick's Day
And I've no damn reason to be in this room, except (to tell

You the truth) for a letter that came with booking and airfare.
The letter came from a private bank in Luxembourg, on Route d'Esch,
I think, and was printed beautifully in blue ink. And there

Was a sepia-tinted etching, too, of soldiers drinking in a guardroom,
From a painting by Gerbrand van den Eeckhout, a bit of Dutch
Art by a competent fellow trained in Rembrandt's studio, I presume –

As smug, no doubt, as any Dutchman with a jug of brandy
And a tobacco pouch can be. Like me, the United Provinces
Were on constant alert, for if it wasn't the Spanish it was the sea;

And, so, my understanding, drawn from the explanatory notes
That accompanied the anonymous gift, is quite simply
That even in times of danger a poet can be lazy and degenerate,
Something readily understood in seventeenth century Holland:

That a gift can be sent to a poet not known outside his native country,
And by a secretive Foundation that deals only in dreams,
Is proof – because proof is needed – that nothing is ever as it seems.

ACKNOWLEDGEMENTS

Thanks to the editors of the following where many of these poems were first published: *Irish Times, PN Review, Poetry Review, Poetry Ireland Review, Southword, New England Review* and *Poems from Pandemia* (Munster Literature Centre), Poetry Encounters, *The Stinging Fly* and *Arena,* RTÉ Radio 1. Grateful acknowledgement is made to The Arts Council of Ireland for their continuing support of Aosdána. Thanks yet again to poet Patrick Cotter for his continuous support over the years, but especially for his heroic efforts to help the Munster writing community during the recent Covid pandemic.

A thousand thanks to those angels of Carcanet Press: to Jazmine and Andrew, to Michael Schmidt and John McAuliffe. I am particularly grateful to John McAuliffe for his early reading of the manuscript and his brilliant editorial suggestions.

And gratitude, with love, to the one and only Catherine Coakley.